# EASY GEOMETRIC PATTERNS

## COLOURING BOOK (VOLUME 2)

L.J. Knight

*Easy Geometric Patterns Colouring Book (Volume 2)* features fifty fun repeating pattern illustrations by L.J. Knight. They're designed to be easy to colour, making them suitable for all ages.

These images can be coloured with pencils, markers and other media. If you use markers, or tend to press heavily on the page, it's helpful to place a sheet of card, scrap paper or plastic under the page you're colouring to protect the image underneath. There is a blank page at the end of the book that you can use for this, or for colour testing.

*Easy Geometric Patterns Colouring Book (Volume 2)* is the 19th title in the *LJK Colouring Books* series. This growing series has hundreds of quality designs for all ages. For more information and free printable sample pages, visit **ljknightart.com/colouring**

First published in February 2021.

#4

#6

#7

#8

#9

#10

#13

#14

#15

#16

#18

#22

#35

#47

# BONUS PAGES

The following pages contain free sample designs
from some of my other colouring books

For more information, visit
ljknightart.com/colouring

*Easy Mandalas Colouring Book*

ljknightart.com/colouring/easy-mandalas

*Magic Mandalas 2 Colouring Book for Kids*

ljknightart.com/colouring/magic-mandalas-2

*Cute and Easy Kawaii Colouring Book - ljknightart.com/colouring/easy-kawaii*

Thank you for buying *Easy Geometric Patterns Colouring Book (Volume 2)*. For more repeating pattern colouring pages, check out the other volumes in the series.

I have a growing range of colouring books for all ages with various themes, which are available from Amazon. For more information, visit **ljknightart.com/colouring**

This page has intentionally been left blank, so you can remove it and place it under the page you're colouring to protect the image underneath, or use it for colour testing. A craft knife is recommended for easy removal.

Printed in Great Britain
by Amazon

45939844R00071